How to ride the waves of life;
that is the greatest challenge for most of us.

We have no control over the waves,
but we can learn to navigate the challenges life brings,
with a surprisingly simple, pure and powerful compass.

Or wait...

Why should you, really?

A way out

- Have you ever felt like life is playing tricks on you, pulling you down, shaking you up so much that you lose all sense of direction, unsure if you're even still alive, as if you're stuck on a rollercoaster?
- Or perhaps nothing seems to be happening at all, life just seems to be passing you by, and you feel like you're not really participating, as if you don't matter?
- Or maybe life is demanding more from you than you feel capable of giving? As if you need to split yourself in two every day just to meet all the expectations?
- Or do you feel like you have so much to offer, so much love to give, but it seems like no one in the world is waiting for you?
- Or does it feel like you have no control over yourself and your life, as if someone or something is running the show, and you're just being carried along?
- Or, or, or...
- Or maybe as you're reading this, your own version of this comes to mind?

Most of us know these kinds of thoughts and feelings.

But hey... there is a WAY OUT.

Think about this for a moment: after every breath, after every inhale and exhale, everything in the universe has changed.

The universe and life have one thing in common, namely that **the only constant is that everything is constantly moving, changing, transforming.**

I wonder, have you ever come across anything that has helped you to deal with this constant unpredictability of life?

If you can answer 'yes', then lucky you. I haven't, so I've had to learn through constant trial and error. What made a difference to me was the discovery of a transformative compass — a magic steering wheel! Learning to steer this magic wheel is, as far as I'm concerned, **the ultimate life skill.**

In this booklet you'll read all about this magic wheel that may be able to help you, just as it helped me. Read this booklet and dive into the wonderful world of transformation; go for it, practice it and keep practicing.

Please, don't just blindly accept my words, but question how the transformation works for you and in your own life. Ultimately, you'll find out for yourself what it is that you need.

The essence

Looking back over the course of my life, it's become clear to me that, if life has taught me anything at all, its greatest lesson has been to teach me to remember who I truly am and how to live accordingly. Life has challenged and taught me to return to my true self.

For me, life is therefore one great masterclass that teaches us to be faithful to our essence, because if we aren't, life will continue to be a challenge.

For me, living from essence means choosing to live in a state of awareness and making conscious decisions based on what is truly good for me. And you can choose that too. We all can, once we learn to recognize our essence.

Learning to live from your essence starts with making time for yourself. Yes, it's as simple as that. It means taking a break from focusing on and interacting with the physical and digital world around you. It means stepping back for a while to create some time to be alone with yourself. This is about you, after all.

It's about you getting closer to yourself; about understanding and getting to the bottom of who you really are. Who you see in the mirror. You'll learn about your deepest motivations: your thoughts, feelings, beliefs, fears, patterns and more.

And you'll ask yourself questions such as: 'What do I really need?', 'Who or what is truly good and healthy for me (and who or what isn't)?', 'What are my deepest desires?'

You'll discover the deep, subconscious forces that drive you. The inner obstacles that are holding you back (even if you're not aware or conscious of any such obstacles). The automatic 'triggers' that shape your life and your contact with other people.

This way, you'll gradually discover how to truly take the best care of yourself (and what you should avoid). Because true self-care is only possible when you deeply understand yourself.

It will enable you to keep a razor-sharp focus on what is truly important and good for you, irrespective of the expectations of those around you. To decide where and in whom to invest your attention, time and energy. And where and in whom not to. This will also make it possible for you, in full awareness, to decide who you will and will not allow into your 'space'. You'll thus set clear boundaries and consciously choose to prioritise your physical, mental, emotional, relational and spiritual well-being.

It's about what's right and healthy for you.

By pausing before making a decision to ensure that it's right for you, you'll find that it'll become increasingly easy to make the right choices.

So find a moment or, better still, several moments, every day just for yourself. Create the time and peace of mind to be with yourself and to engage with yourself. You can do this in a favourite space in your home or on the couch, or by doing something on your own that you enjoy or have always thought you'd like to try.

It's about finding your own path; alone or with like-minded people with whom you can share valuable thoughts. Build a life that fulfils you, your soul, with joy, pleasure and a deep sense of fulfilment.

Sound good?

Then the next question is:

HOW
can you transition from your current life to a life lived from your essence?

But first: be your own guru

These are days of great unrest in all walks of life.
– Harriette Curtiss (1856-1932), 'The Key to the Universe'

This statement is in the foreword of a book from 1915 and probably applies to many times and places. The fact is, life is a risky business, that has always been the case. Life has something in store for all of us. Everyone is on a journey, each of us with our own challenges, desires and fundamental questions about life. Many of us search for wisdom, knowledge, and answers to life's fundamental questions, striving to make the best of it That's as true now as it was 2,500 years ago.

In our search, we often turn to others for inspiration and guidance. It is important to realize that this can make us vulnerable — susceptible to people who claim to have all the answers and prone to accepting their opinions and advice about what's right for us and what we need. But what if you follow their advice, and your life still doesn't come close to your ideal? Because you face challenges that get in the way. How does that make you feel?

Life is *not* something you can control. After all:

Life is what happens to us while we are making other plans.
– Allen Saunders (1899-1986), 'Reader's digest' (1957)

Yet this is the opposite of what lifestyle influencers and success gurus would have you believe. Namely, that you have full control over the 'design' of your life — provided, of course, that you follow their tips.

In my practice, I've seen that it is precisely these kinds of messages that make people — both young and old — feel unhappy and inadequate. Because their own lives feel worlds apart from the successful, popular, wealthy and seemingly happy lives of the influencers and gurus they admire.

The reality is, life throws all sorts of things at us that we don't want and, conversely, it doesn't always give us what we do want. In Buddhist teachings, these are regarded as the two main sources of suffering.

The only thing we can influence is how we deal with this and the choices we make. But that isn't so easy if you come up against all sorts of major challenges throughout your life.

Instead of offering tips or quick answers, this book provides a practice that helps you discover yourself and find the answers within. It's a process you can explore on your own or together with a friend.

Safe travels

But don't forget that *shiny influencers, derailed gurus and false prophets* only show a small part of themselves. And above all, remember: they don't genuinely care about your well-being, health, success or happiness. Keep in mind: you are often just a means to *their* end.

So, to travel safely on your journey through transitions in yourself and in your life:

- Don't simply believe everything you hear; examine everything within yourself.
- Many answers to your questions are hidden deep inside you: this journey will teach you how to bring those answers to the surface and to learn to listen to what you know, deep down, to be true.
- Sincere education nurtures your inner strength and increases your independence.
- The 'lessons' in this book will provide you with the foundation and key tools to achieve this.

So that this puts you on the path of what works for you!

As a rule of thumb:

**Believe nothing,
 investigate everything.**

**Reject nothing,
 integrate everything.**

(And — take 'nothing' and 'everything' with a pinch of salt. It's about the idea, it's not set in stone!)

Let's start with an exercise.
Give it your full focus.
First read the instructions, then carry them out.

Sit comfortably, up straight, feel your inner strength.

Close your eyes and focus on your belly.
If it helps, place a hand on your belly to help you focus.

Feel your in and out breath; the gentle expansion of your belly as you inhale and the relaxation as you exhale.

Let your breath become longer, deeper and slower.

Feel present, feel strong.
Feel comfortable and relaxed.

And when you're ready:
look at the diagram on the next page and slowly repeat, either out loud or to yourself, the words:

I AM THE WORK

Let the words resonate within you,
until you can feel their vibration within your body.

Life's real work isn't the work that pays the bills.
That's just a means to an end.

Life's real work is

YOU!

Your real work is
your personal health:

**physical
mental
emotional
relational
spiritual**

'Εννέα' is Greek for nine

The magic wheel consists of nine points on a circle that you navigate through in every complete transformation.

The true full name for this magic wheel is therefore actually the **'EnneaFlow Transformative Process Model*'**.

This represents a process that unfolds or flows through nine points — hence 'ennea'. According to this philoscphy, a complete process consists of ten phases (ten because the circle begins and ends at point 9). The key point here is that there are natural laws ('forces') which impact every process of change. These forces influence how processes unfold, how one thing leads to another and ensure that such a process flows — or comes to a halt.

You may well recognise these phases as you read further in this book. However, until now, you were probably unaware of how these natural laws are interconnected; things just seemed to happen to you, as if by chance. Do you recognise this?

The magic wheel works so simply and yet so powerfully! You'll experience this once you learn to work with it consciously. This model spins and moves like a magic wheel. Just as everything

---

* Coaching and Counselling to the Point, 2021, p. 74

around you spins and moves. Think of the universe, the Earth and the planets; after all, you're a part of it.

With this magic wheel in your hands, you'll soon be able to consciously navigate through the various phases of transformation. This book will teach you to consciously 'process' each phase, both within yourself and in your encounters with the outside world.

Each phase is unique. Each phase calls for something different: a different focus, a different practice. By completing the exercises in this book, you'll learn to navigate through these various phases. With some practise, you'll soon be able to recognise which phase is at play in a particular moment or in any particular situation. And soon you'll also know what action you need to take.

But don't forget, this will only work if you fully focus on every single phase and in full honestly do the task that each phase requires. If you try to take a short cut or even skip a phase, you won't get the full benefits. There's an ancient wisdom hidden in this magic wheel that says that a transformative process will stagnate or even stop altogether if a phase isn't fully or sincerely addressed.

So, if something's bothering you, or your inner journey is faltering, return to the model. You can always come back to it to see which phase you're at. And then check whether there's a phase that you didn't focus on properly. By returning to that phase, you'll find that your journey will start flowing again and you'll be able to move forward once more.

You'll find that the more you practice, the easier it'll get and the more powerful this seemingly simple model will become for you.

Curious?

The magic wheel

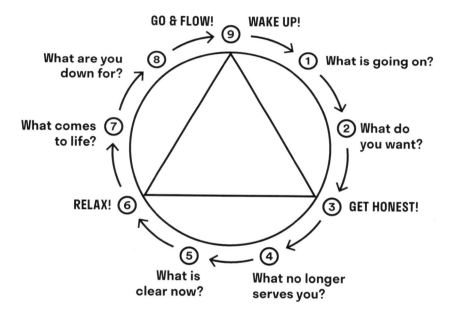

But before we get started...

We'll soon start going through the ten phases together, step by step. We'll stop at each phase for you to read what it entails. Then you'll dive into the questions that will help you explore what that phase means to you.

But before we start, here are a few important key principles. These are your beacons of light to give you guidance, direction and focus during your journey.

- Just as in the universe, everything is in constant flux — in you, in your life and in the world around you. With each breath in and each breath out 'the world' has changed. Whether you're aware of it or not; this is how it is.

- Transformations can be both changes, desired or undesired, arising from events in the outside world, as well as transformations that you wish for and initiate yourself.

- To practise using *the magic wheel,* think of a situation or change process in your life. This can be something that's happening to you right now or something from your past. The specific 'case' you choose doesn't matter.

- The description of each phase is followed by questions related to 'the work' required in that phase. These questions will help you to reflect what you're dealing with at that point.

- The questions are formulated as generally as possible, so focus on those questions that are relevant to you and the specific situation you're facing. And at any one of the phases, other questions may come to mind; formulate and answer the questions that are most relevant to you.

- Use **My IATW Journal** (which complements this book) or your own preferred notebook. Jot down useful insights, exercises and thoughts; re-read them later or add new insights as they come.

- Even if you're not much of a writer, you'll be doing yourself a great favour by writing down your answers in your notebook, devoting at least a page to each phase. Your notebook will thus become a valuable and 'living' logbook which you can refer back to and add to, again and again.

- A music track has been composed to accompany each point on the magic wheel. Each phase requires different work which brings or requires a different energy, thought or feeling. Music can support you in this process. You can explore whether this works for you.

- Try listening to the track accompanying a phase before answering its questions and let the music sink in first. Or perhaps for you it's better to first reflect on the questions in the phase and then listed to the track. What matters is finding what works for you.

- Although we'll be going through the ten phases of *the magic wheel* in order, as you become familiar with the model, you can move through the phases in any order and focus on what's relevant for you at that moment.

- The most important thing is that you work on whatever phase is relevant for you in that moment or which suddenly gives you some gain insights. You can simply move back and forth between the phases until you feel that you've got everything clear and worked out.

- You can also do this exercise with a friend, partner or colleague; with anyone you feel comfortable with and who can help you to move on. You can also help each other to progress and grow.

- Learning about the ten phases in any transformational process can be a real gamechanger. Just think, soon you'll easily recognise each of these ten phases in any situation or relationship and be able to say; 'Oh, hold on, this is just phase 4' or 'This is phase 6!'. And once you recognise which phase you're in, you'll also know what action to take.

- Treat and approach this process like a game; playfully learning to live more consciously and to play with life as life plays with you. Or as a dance, with your own life as your dancing partner: you learn the steps, follow the rhythm and together you find flow and harmony.

- Like everything, the more often you engage and practice, the more attention, time and energy you invest, the more you'll get out of it and the more skilled you'll become.

Importantly: if you notice that your process is stalling, take some time to calmly revisit the previous phases. There might be a phase that you haven't fully engaged with or where you haven't answered the questions thoroughly. It could be a phase that, due to personal preferences, you were less inclined to give your full attention to — we all have those. Often, this is the reason why processes slow down or come to a stop.

And finally: read this book 3 times!

- The first time just browse to see what it's about.

- The second time with focused attention to really understand and practice the work.

- The third time thoroughly, to really make it your own and master it.

So, what are you waiting for? Just dive in, and you'll see how it starts to work for you.

Hey you! Wake up!

The road to CONSCIOUSNESS

Our journey begins at the top of the circle at point 9. This is where the EnneaFlow Transformative Process Method begins. Point 9 symbolises 'being at rest': life plods along, meandering ever onwards irrespective of whether the experiences are welcome or not. It's as if your life is on autopilot, following fixed routines without much thought but simply accepting what and how they are. It's not a question of whether you're happy about this, it's just the way it is, day in, day out. And even if you're not really happy about it, you can't see a 'way out'; this is apparently what life's like so you keep going, day in, day out. UNTIL...

Hold on! Let's first take a short break for an exercise:

> Feel your feet on the ground. Close your eyes for a moment.
>
> Straighten your back, don't slouch, sit straight, feel the strength in your back.
> Let your breath become slower, longer and deeper. In... out...
> Relax the muscles in your neck and shoulders.
> Let all the tension fall away.
> Relax your face, smile.
> Take a short moment for yourself. Just sit and 'be' for a while.
>
> Don't read on until you've enjoyed a moment of real calm with yourself.
>
> Take three deep, powerful, intense breaths.
> Then let the following question sink in:
>
> **'What the f*ck is the MEANING of my life?'**

Maybe something comes to mind, maybe not.
That's often the case with exercises like this and it's fine.

Does one of the following statements resonate with you? Does one of them apply to you? If not, how would you rephrase any of these statements?

- Life seems to be passing me by; I'm overwhelmed by all the options available to me and I can't choose, join in or take action.

- My life seemed to be on course, going the way I wanted it to, but then something happened and I suddenly feel as if I'm in free fall, as if the ground is falling away from under my feet.
- Every day I try to meet the never-ending demands and expectations put on me by the outside world; I often feel empty, like a squeezed-out lemon, but what do I actually want? I don't really know.
- I have everything I could possibly desire. And yet at times I feel somewhat empty, lost, even dissatisfied. Why is that? Do I perhaps feel guilty? Because, after all, I have such a good and easy life compared to others; I have absolutely no reason not to feel happy.
- I'm totally happy, living in harmony with what I deep down feel I'm alive for.

The problem with living 'on autopilot' is that it's our greatest source of suffering AND we're usually stuck there without even being aware of it. When we're 'trapped' we tell ourselves the same stories again and again; we simply can't see a way out. Well, living 'on autopilot' is the perfect recipe for feeling trapped, directionless, empty, burned out, redundant or simply utterly mundane. And what's the point of that?

It's this very suffering that can awaken us from our sleeping state.

Think about it; why would you want to come out of your stupor if the stupor feels fine and safe? Or why change when it's only the thought of Friday afternoon and the weekend that gets you through the working week? You wouldn't, right?

Unless something or someone gives you a rough 'wake-up call' and you suddenly see the truth. Or if the price of living 'on autopilot' becomes palpably too high and you can no longer pull it off. Or life itself confronts you with a crisis: a broken heart, for example, or the loss of a loved one, job or home. Or if someone you trusted completely cheats on you. Because you were asleep and unaware of what was going on. But:

Every crisis is a wake-up call!

In the world of spiritual growth, waking up is the first and most crucial step on the journey. Point 9 symbolises the beginning of a transformation process. Without a wake-up call there's no journey, no growth, no transformation. It's as simple as that. So, here's how it works:

You sleep — you suffer —
this suffering wakes you up — and BAM!

Your journey begins.

Or rather... your journey begins only

IF you decide that it should.

After all, you can also simply turn over and go back to sleep, look away, ignore the unpleasant feeling and pretend that nothing's wrong. That's what most people do.

So, what will you do?

Ask yourself:

- For what or whom was (or am) I 'asleep'?

- What sorts of things do I tend to overlook? Or what have I possibly overlooked or ignored for a long time?

- What numbs me and causes me to go on autopilot?

- In which situations; where, when causes me to fall 'asleep' and go on autopilot?

- What's at the heart of my struggles or suffering? What's it about? What am I avoiding?

- How am I on autopilot?

- What signals indicate that I'm numb and on autopilot?

- What or who triggered my wake-up call?

- Why did this wake me up?

- What did this wake-up call make me realise?

- What have I woken up to or become aware of?

What is going on?

The road to EXPLORATION

Did you wake up gently at point 9? Or with a start? Then you've released energy. Energy that can help or 'prompt' you to explore. Once startled into wakefulness, you may suddenly start asking yourself: 'What's actually going on here?', 'What's happening?', 'What's the problem?' and so on. When this happens, it means you've arrived at point 1.

Point 1 symbolises the exploration phase. In this phase you're going to take a close look at the situation you're in. You might feel as though you're sailing through a storm, desperately searching for a place of shelter where you can get a hold on the chaos around you and some clarity about what's happening.

What you're doing at point 1 is rousing your inner Sherlock Holmes. It may be useful in this phase to have a friend, sibling or coach to help you with this detective work. Because it's crucial to get as clear an understanding as possible of what is at the core of your problem or challenge. About the factors that are at play. To achieve this, you first need a thorough and complete overview of the whole situation; you need to 'see the whole elephant in the room'. Something 'must' change, but what?

The first step is look outside yourself, to ask the right questions and map out all the details. You may need to look back to 'when everything was fine', to the root of where and how 'it' started, to make a timeline of events, what the other person did or said, how you reacted, what you said, what you did or didn't do and so on. Looking back, you may suddenly see the importance of certain events or actions that didn't seem important at the time. So the aim of this phase is to get a clear overview of the whole situation; it's a continuous dance between:

Zooming in on the details.
Zooming out to get the full picture.

All too often our gut reaction here is to point the finger at others, at the outside world. We tend to zoom in on what others have or haven't done or said. Because it's so easy (and comfortable) to ignore and disregard our own role. But here's the thing: ultimately, recognising your own role, your own part-however difficult that may be-is the true gamechanger. Just remember:

> You can only change that
> which you see in yourself.
> Any blind spot, anything you deny,
> will control you and your life.

Acknowledging your own role is a powerful step. By only seeing problems as originating from the outside risks making you feel powerless. Or even of being victimised because, of course, you can't control those things that are outside of you.

Acknowledging your own role can be a bitter pill to swallow, but doing so puts you in control. This journey is therefore certainly not a 'walk in the park'. It requires real courage and discipline.

You might need to probe the depths of your mind: your fears, your deepest longings and facets of your character that have so far remained hidden. Because:

Once you recognise it, you can see it.
Once you understand it, you can act upon it.
Once you master it, you can be it.

One of the first things you need to understand is that your ego is always chasing an 'idealised self-image'. You're probably not even aware of it, but subconsciously we're all constantly working towards our idealised self-image.

An image you probably don't even know you have of yourself. It's who you deep down think you must be in order to be worthy of being seen, heard, appreciated and loved. To belong.

> **TEST   Do any of these statements ring true?**
>
> ☐ I'm a good person; I always try hard to do the right thing.
> ☐ I'm a kind person; I want to be caring towards others.
> ☐ I'm a competent person; pursuing success and being successful gives me energy.
> ☐ I'm an exceptional person; I'm searching for what really matters in life.
> ☐ I approach things rationally; I thrive on objective facts and knowledge.
> ☐ I'm a cautious person; I recognise the risks so am always well prepared.
> ☐ I love freedom, fun and surprises; I always see alternatives.
> ☐ I'm a steadfast person; I like to make an impact and challenge others.
> ☐ I'm a relaxed and content person; what I like most is a peaceful and harmonious life.

Ask yourself:

- Which factors or people do I see as the cause of the situation, challenge or crisis?

- If I create a timeline of the situation, challenge, or crisis, what would it look like?

- How am I contributing, or how have I contributed, to this situation, challenge or crisis? What was or is my role in it?

- What did I say or do? Or what did I fail to say or do?

- Are there specific topics, situations or people that particularly trigger me?

- When I am triggered, what is my automatic reaction, both internally and externally?

- What are my strengths and skills? What do I find difficult? Or where do I fall short?

- How do I describe my idealised self-image? What am I unconsciously striving for in terms of how others see me?

- If I take a step back, is there a connection between pursuing my idealised self-image and the situation, challenge or crisis, and if so, what is it?

What do you want?

The road to WILLPOWER

After your analysis and overview at point 1, you'll move on to point 2. Once we have a full picture of what's going on, the focus shifts to questions such as 'What do you really want from this?', 'What is really important to you?', 'What do you really need?', 'What is really good or healthy for you?' and 'What are your needs, wants and desires?'. Here again we can often use another person's help to clarify the answers to these questions.

Because it's no easy thing to truly recognise and understand your needs and desires. You need to be in touch with your body and your instincts. Many of us have lost that connection. This may be due to our upbringing, not only by our parents but also by our environment and school. Many of us were taught to suppress our feelings and prioritise what the outside world said was 'right'. This has made us sensitive to the expectations of others.

Do you remember the impulses you felt as a child? Many of us were told to ignore them; to sit still when our bodies wanted to move or play, or to be quiet when we wanted to laugh, cry, shout or sing. We picked up the message that we weren't 'good' children if we gave in to our own needs, impulses or ideas. And this caused us to develop limiting beliefs. Does this sound familiar to you?

For many of us, these experiences played a role in suppressing our true selves This is probably true for you too. Perhaps you were also taught (and even encouraged) to disregard your impulses and emotions. To distance yourself from feeling what YOU really wanted and needed. Instead, you conformed, allowed yourself to be led by the expectations of others and subconsciously prioritised pleasing them. This may even be true of people you love very much — your parents, a partner or your friends, for example.

It's so much easier to prioritise the plans and wishes of others rather than your own desires and needs. It's not that others necessarily ask you to do that or demand (too) much of you; it's simply that you find it difficult to stand up for yourself. You let yourself down and demand too much of yourself. The resulting suffering ultimately pushes you to focus on yourself.

You have to learn to recognise your true needs and to prioritise them; to really take good care of yourself — physically, mentally, emotionally, relationally and spiritually. This isn't an indulgence, it's a necessity, something you owe yourself. And remember, it's your responsibility to look after yourself, not other people's.

Now you may genuinely believe that you're taking good care of yourself. And in many ways you probably are. However, your suffering, your feeling of being unfulfilled, is a sign. A sign that reflects back to you that you sometimes sell yourself short. That there are areas in which you neglect or maybe even forget your own needs. This may be because you don't realise that these are areas that are deeply important to you.

Taking true care of yourself is only possible if you truly know yourself.

This includes an understanding of your true wants and desires, of what you really need, maybe even the true meaning of your life.

Working through this phase at point 2 may well unleash a willpower in you that you've never felt before, certainly never this powerfully.

It's the willpower you use to say: 'I won't let that happen to me again.' 'From now on, I'll stand firm behind my decisions and stick to my plans.' 'From now on, I'll focus on recognising and protecting my boundaries.' 'I'll not be distracted and be fully focused on what I really want in life.'

So it's high time to check in with:

YOUR WILL!

Remember how you were as a child: what were the times that you felt good and what was it that made you feel so good?

Think about how you were, what you did, where you were and how your body took care of you, about how meeting your own needs came naturally, before you started allowing yourself to be led by the wishes and demands of others. Reconnect with your impulses, stamp your feet and voice your desires.

Do you feel that passion? That's you, reconnecting with yourself!

Ask yourself:

- Deep down, what is truly important to me?
  In my relationships? In my work? In my life?

- What are my true dreams and ambitions?
  Or did I have in the past?

- What is the main obstacle to realising my dreams or ambitions?

- What do I truly long for?
  What are my real needs?

- How are my needs being met? And how are they not?
  Or how do I provide for my own needs? And how not?

- What do I want? And what do I really not want? Also in relation to the situation, challenge or crisis of my case?

- What or who is keeping me from what I want?
  Or conversely, by what or whom do I allow myself to be held captive in what I really don't want?

- To what extent, with what and how do I take good care of myself? And how and with what could I take better care of myself?

- If I could change something in myself or my life with a magic wand, what would it be?

Hey you! Get honest!

The road to TRANSPARENCY

Following on from your explorations at point 1 and 2, you move on to point 3: the second shock point. 'The second shock point?' you're probably asking yourself, 'Was there a first one then?'

Yes, the first shock point was at point 9, at the start of this process, when you got your wake-up call. We call them shock points because this is where the energy that makes the magic wheel of transformation turn enters your system. Or not, and the process simply comes to a halt. So, after 'Wake up!' at point 9, the second shock point is at point 3: 'Be honest!' At this point, there is a (great) risk that the process will slow down, stagnate or even come to a complete stillstand.

Because what often happens after point 2 — it's such a human reaction — is that we start to kid ourselves, or justify the situation with arguments such as, **'Actually, the advantages outweigh the disadvantages.' 'He/she doesn't really mean it.' Or that 'Despite everything, a lot of things are going just fine.'**

I call these our 'self-justifications'. They allow you keep things as they are even though, if you're truly honest with yourself, you know deep down that they're not really, even really not, true.

This is a self-protection mechanism that kicks in when we know, deep down, that being truly honest with ourselves will have consequences. And we usually don't want or dare to face those consequences because doing so will mean that we have to step outside the safety of our comfort zone or discard those things that we're attached to.

This protective mechanism may have been triggered precisely because, at point 2, we were able to vent our hearts to a friend or therapist, for example. After all, a good chat can help us to see the bright side again and we can (and want to) move forward with the situation in which we find ourselves.

Does this ring true?

And reflect on this for a moment: what's your 'self-justification' to avoid following up on what's bothering you or on what you truly need? How do you try to make things seem better than they actually are? So that you can avoid the repercussions that are inevitable if you're honest with yourself?

At this point, we all too often and for far too long choose to delude ourselves because we're unwilling or don't dare to deal with the consequences of being truly honest with ourselves (and others). After all, it's often so much easier to kid ourselves and bury our heads in the sand than it is to face reality. And as a result, the change process stagnates. The problem, however, is that simply not wanting to know, see or hear something, doesn't make it disappear. On the contrary, those things we deny reside and remain shadowed within us, forming hidden motivators that continue to restrict and imprison us.

Unless we face reality and realise that, in reality, we have no other choice. Or someone steadfastly holds up a mirror for us. Or others make choices that have consequences for us. These are just three examples of an 'outside shock', but there are many others. Whatever the context, once we take our heads out of the sand and stop behaving as if nothing's wrong, in phase 3 we'll be forced to a standstill.

We take a step back at this shock point and make time to become truly honest with ourselves. We do this by asking ourselves questions such as: 'What am I really doing?' 'What am I really afraid of?' 'What do I really think and hope to achieve with this?' 'Is that thing that I'm so resolutely pursuing really good for me?' And so on. There is little that is more confronting than removing the veils that cover our inner self, forcing us to face our true selves. But:

Only the truth about ourselves can set us free.

– Claudio Naranjo (1932-2019)

Now's the time to tackle this deception — this self-deception. This isn't so much about the deliberate lies or half-truths that we might tell others; it's about the stories we tell ourselves, the ones we want to believe, that we've become attached to and want — subconsciously — to hold on to.

These stories, that we so desperately want to believe, are also the result of the pursuit of our idealised self-image. It's about who we think we must be to be worthy of being loved. And to be seen, heard, appreciated, to belong. It's why we're so attached to this self-image and why it can feel so vitally important.

And it's this attachment to our idealised self-image that keeps us imprisoned in certain situations, relationships and so on. To free ourselves from this attachment, we have to learn to truly understand ourselves and the workings of our ego.

Yes, because that's exactly what our idealized self-image is:

our ego.

And in this work, we don't identify just one 'kind' of ego, but nine ('ennea') distinct ego versions or character structures, each fundamentally different in nature, content and function.

Want to find out more?

Ego

Time to dive deep into our ego! But what does that actually mean?

The ego represents our self-identification and how we see, or want to see, ourselves in relation to the world around us. It's the obstacle that separates us from our true self. It's the masks we wear, the roles we play. It's also the obstacle between ourselves and others, between how we'd like to live/work and how we actually live/work.

Our self-deception sustains our ego with those stories and ideas about ourselves that we're so attached to. Attached, because deep down we're convinced that we need them, that we can't do without them. It's this cognitive delusion that we mean by self-deception. Self-deception refers to our ego-driven perspectives that are like the blinkers through which we look at the outside world, at others and at ourselves, but through which we can see only a fraction of the whole picture.

Our ego subconsciously and automatically focuses our attention on those things that, without being fully aware of it, we consider to be truly important. Conversely, it quickly, subconsciously and automatically filters out those things that are less important or even to irrelevant to it. Our blinkers only let through that information that we focus our attention on. We're not even aware of these blinkers and therefore not aware of how they limit and colour what we see. It takes practice, effort and, above all, the desire and ability to be honest with ourselves to become aware of this, to see it.

The exploration of the working of the ego, and thus of our self-deception, begins with the realisation that our ego is always 'hungry' and looking for food with which to satisfy this hunger. 'Ego food' includes affirmation, recognition, appreciation, admiration, security, control, making an impact and so on. The problem with this ego hunger is that it's never fully or permanently satisfied; like the hungry caterpillar, it remains unfulfilled and hungry. Broadly speaking, our 'ego food' falls into three main categories of inner urges:

1. **Recognition:** this relates to universal human needs such as being seen, heard, liked, valued, recognised, respected and loved and feeling a sense of belonging. There might be a tension between the desire to be true to ourselves and the desire to be seen, heard, liked and so on by others.

2. **Possessiveness:** this relates to our universal human concern for survival. It stems from our natural fear of not having access to what we need when we need it; be this material resources, security or emotional support.

3. **Dominance:** this relates to the universal human need to protect ourselves and exert control over our environment, others and, primarily, ourselves. It stems from our innate desire to ensure our safety and secure that which we think we need from those around us.

You may now be thinking: 'This isn't me; this isn't about me.' You may not always recognise these urges, but don't be fooled: they're there, subtly steering your choices. So, the question isn't 'if' they're at work in you, but rather 'how' they're at work in you. They're deeply rooted and shape our behaviour and interactions. But once we recognise and acknowledge them, we can choose to take a different path.

A tool to really get to know yourself

As you now know, 'Ennea' is Greek for nine; however, the circle with 9 points offers a second tool, called the Enneagram. This model distinguishes 9 character or ego structures and describes them on a deep level. This makes it easier to get to know and understand yourself more deeply and at a faster pace.

For an introduction to the 9 Enneagram types or points, you can play a game to discover your type: the 'What's My Point?' game.

What's My Point?
Play the game and discover yourself!

Ask yourself:

- What is my deepest ego hunger; what is it about?

- What kind of ego food am I actually trying to obtain? From whom, and how do I try to obtain it?

- If I'm really honest with myself: how do the three urges play out in me? What is this about for me?

- What behaviour does this lead to in the external world?

- Which of my thoughts, emotions, habits or tendencies do I find difficult to acknowledge and try to hide from myself and others?

- How do I tend to make things look better than they are?

- If I'm really honest with myself: does the other person(s) also have another side (negative or positive) that I would prefer to deny, not see and ignore?

- What would I prefer to sweep under the rug? What do I avoid facing?

- If I'm really honest with myself: how do I keep the situation, challenge or crisis alive?

- Which consequences would I prefer to avoid or not face?

Let go

The road to PROCESSING

As a result of being truly and deeply honest with yourself at point 3, you move on to point 4. Many of us may have quite a lot to process here. Because let's face it, being honest about yourself and your contribution to the situation that you're dealing with, as you were at point 3, is no small thing. Point 4 is all about processing; including all those painful emotions that may have surfaced in the previous phase. But this phase is also about letting go of those things that at point 3 you identified as no longer serving you. And that can be a difficult and painful process.

Let's start by taking a step back: you now understand your own part in the situation you're currently dealing with, or at least your role in perpetuating it. A deep understanding of our true selves shatters our idealised self-image. We're confronted with how we're driven and controlled by our ego cravings. The inner struggle that this can produce is often referred to as the 'dark night of the soul'. But remember that dawn follows even the darkest night (and that we're still only at point 4 in the process).

Point 4 represents a difficult phase for many of us because it entails a sort of internal spring cleaning. It's where we have a good clean out and purge ourselves and our lives of those things that no longer serve us. Most people would prefer to avoid the pain this causes and thus eschew this phase. Yet this phase is unavoidable, necessary, healing and ultimately liberating on the path to growth and transformation. And remember that anything you avoid dealing with now, you'll carry with you into your future. So while pausing here may be painful and difficult, this too is temporary, and ultimately we all appreciate a good clean out.

Our work at point 4 involves processing emotions, digesting pain, mourning loss. It involves letting go of all those things that no longer serve us: things such as beliefs or habits (both about ourselves and about the outside world) that may limit us, relationships, situations or patterns that we're stuck in, stories we keep telling ourselves and others, memories we keep returning to and so on. It's about letting go of those things we've been carrying around for so long but that hurt us, scare us, make us angry, things that keep us small or hold us back. In short, everything that no longer serves us.

From a young age, we all subconsciously and instinctively build walls around ourselves, walls that protect us from the outside world and, especially, from feeling emotional pain.

By taking this path towards awareness and conscious living, we'll increasingly discover and experience that these walls don't only offer protection — they also come at a price.

Because every time we hold back to avoid feeling pain, we're also holding back our free-flowing life force. And that can eventually make us ill. These instinctive protective reactions may shelter us from pain, they also prevent us from feeling truly happy, spontaneous or joyful. That protective wall is standing between us and our true selves. And between us and others.

So it's important to realise that your strategy to protect yourself can actually be getting in the way of your personal development and happiness. And can in fact keep you removed from your deepest desires.

Here's a great exercise to deal with those emotions that may arise during this process: take a moment and allow yourself to experience them in full. Be patient, gentle and kind to yourself; examine your emotions, without judgement; accept them, talk to them, be curious about what your emotions are trying to tell you or what they're truly about. Take your time and focus and you'll find that they'll melt away like snow in the sun.

This is a key to inner healing and to ultimate freedom.

As children we're often taught to hide our emotions: don't be angry, come back when you've calmed down, stop crying, don't be such a scaredy-cat, don't make such a fuss. Does this ring true?

But emotions are absolutely fine, there's nothing wrong with them, they're part of who we are. They make us human. In fact, expressing emotions is healthy and stops us from building up ever more stress.

Before we move on, there's just one more thing we have to do in this phase and that's to forgive ourselves. We stumble and fall, but we also get up again. So take a deep breath and say the following to yourself:

**It's time to free myself
from everything
that no longer serves me.**

Ask yourself:

- Now that I have been honest with myself in phase 3: what are my attachments about?

- What illusions about myself do I now see through?

- What 'excuses for myself' have I now uncovered?

- What am I saying goodbye to:
  - From what? From whom?
  - Which habits no longer serve me?
  - Which thoughts and beliefs no longer serve me?
  - Which patterns, in myself, in my life or in my relationships, no longer serve me?

- What emotions and thoughts has this process of letting go triggered?

- What pain do I have to process and digest here?

- In what ways can I feel healing as I release these attachments?

- What do I blame myself for, and how can I choose to view this differently?

- What can and will I forgive myself for?

The void

After processing and casting off those things that no longer serve you at point 4, you move into a void between points 4 and 5. This feels like a well-earned rest. You're on the cusp between what's behind you and what will come next. There's an open space between points 4 and 5 on the magic wheel; this open space is also known as 'the void'.

Have you ever cried so hard that everything else seemed to fade away? And that eventually a moment came when you cried your last tear? After which you experienced an unexpected stillness, a peace and a feeling of space? And that it felt, just maybe, as if the sun was suddenly shining again? That's how you'll feel if you worked through and completed the phase at point 4.

Whereas phase 9 is seen as the point of maximum integration — you'll learn more about this at the end of the journey — 'the void' is seen as the point of maximum disintegration.

As if you're in limbo for a while. Because you've cast off and processed so much at point 4 but not yet replaced it with anything else. It's as if you're at the bottom of the ocean. Sitting in silence for a while as the turbulent waves of life rage on far above and beyond you.

Just for a moment there's an emptiness.

It's time to take a step back: you've climbed mountains, weathered storms and maybe even cast out some demons. And when the storm clouds lift, what remains is a serene emptiness. A clarity like no other, and you feel free of those obstacles and ties that used to hold you back.

The emptiness in this phase is like a wonderful and necessary interval between letting go of the old and embracing the new start that awaits you at point 5. It's an essential pit stop. Embrace it. Cherish it. And most importantly, trust it.

You may feel as if you're standing on the edge of something new, something special; in a space where the possibilities are endless but where you don't need to do anything just yet. It's in this emptiness that the real transformation is already beginning to unfold, under the surface and unnoticed.

For now, take a break.

Focus on something else for a while: maybe take a walk or go to the gym. In short, chill out and relax, take some time for yourself.

Take stock

The road to CLARITY

Once you've lingered for long enough in inner silence and emptiness, you return naturally to a sense of awareness. It's the same as after a good night's sleep–as morning comes you wake up naturally and return to consciousness. You feel refreshed and bright again, ready for a new day. In just the same way, we'll progress naturally on to the next phase at point 5. It's as if the fog in your mind has lifted and the obstacles and heaviness of your emotions in your heart have disappeared.

Stripped at point 4 of unhelpful thoughts and no longer burdened with feelings that only get in our way, at point 5 we experience the peace, space and clarity that enables us to take a fresh and unclouded look at where we are.

Incredibly, the earlier chaos now looks very different and uncluttered. What at first seemed so difficult to unravel, too big or complex to oversee, suddenly seems to fall into place. Amazed, we ask ourselves, **'What was so difficult about that?' 'How come I didn't see this before?'**

Arriving at this point, everything suddenly looks so simple. Do you recognise this? Are you maybe experiencing it right now?

Our work in phase 5 involves rational thinking, getting the facts straight (again) and opening the gateway to solutions. This is the time to look back at our journey from our awakening at point 9 to where we are now. To evaluate, take a step back and understand where we are, before we're truly ready to look ahead.

As we do so, we start the process of putting things in order. Because only now that we're no longer so controlled by our emotions (or maybe even our ego), now that they no longer cloud our judgement, do we have a clear view of the situation (the crisis or problem) and can we observe it neutrally and from some distance. We now have the space to think clearly.

Everything falls into place and the solutions suddenly seem obvious. There are suddenly more paths open to you than you could at first have imagined.

My mantra for work on point 5 is therefore:

**Keep your mind clear and stable,
Keep your heart open and warm,
Keep your body relaxed and solid.**[*]

You may be wondering: 'Explore the situation and see the bigger picture — didn't we do that at point 1?' Yes and no. No, because our work at point 5 is different since we find ourselves in a different phase in the process. Yes, because at point 1 we also focused on the big picture, only then it was all about a first exploration. This is called 'divergent thinking': first we collect all the information and details that we think might be relevant, including any examples arising from our emotions. 'Divergent' at point 1 means increase; the point at which we bring more and more into focus.

At point 5, we bring everything back to the essence of the story or problem; this is what's known as 'convergent thinking'. We can do this because the emotions we experienced at point 4 have been absorbed and no longer have the upper hand. We can now rationally organise all the details into to what is and isn't relevant and can distinguish the main issue from the less relevant. We have an overview.

'Convergent thinking' is a process of filtering out all the unnecessary and irrelevant information so that only the pertinent facts and elements remain. And solutions are suddenly able to come to the fore.

---

[*] Enneagram voor Dummies, 2020, p. 196

Ask yourself:

- Where am I now?

- What do I see and think when I look back at where I was when I started this journey at point 9 with 'Waking up'?

- What do I see and think when I look back at the journey I have taken from point 9 up to here?

- What do I now see clearly that I couldn't see or comprehend before?

- What's the bigger picture when I zoom out from here?

- What options or choices do I now see and feel that I didn't see and feel before?

- What solutions do I see now?

- Which unhelpful thoughts/beliefs am I aware of now?

- What helpful thoughts/beliefs am I putting in their place?

- What short phrase or word can help me to keep reminding myself of this?

- What else can I do to help myself remember?

Hey, you! Relax!

The road to COURAGE

Relax your 'abreactions'! Relax my what?

With the solutions from point 5 in hand, the transition now seems like a done deal. Well, hold on for just a minute. Do you remember the shock points at points 9 and 3? Well, here's the third one. And as was the case in point 3, the shock point at point 6 can also slow the process down, cause it to stagnate and even grind to a halt. Let me explain what's happening here.

The essence of this phase is as follows. The solutions we came up with at point 5 are rational solutions; solutions that, unfortunately, more often than not don't reflect our natural behaviour. After all, if it had been in our nature to deal with a situation or problem in this rational way from the start, we wouldn't have had to travel along this path from point 9 to find it. We would have instinctively acted or reacted that way from the start.

Our true nature is how we act, react and see things without really thinking about it. So in a way that feels obvious and that falls within our comfort zone. In the course of our lives we also learn how to act, react and see things differently, in ways that aren't in line with our nature. They fall outside what we're used to.

At point 6 we're going to imagine or visualise what it might be like to actually put the solutions we came up with into practice. Just the thought of doing something that lies outside our nature, and thus our comfort zone, can trigger a physical reaction.

For example: imagine that the solution you came up with at point 5 was to have a conversation with someone you've always found rather difficult to approach and stressful to talk to. The solution seems so simple, but it's not if it's the very thing that lies outside your natural reaction and comfort zone. Is this how you feel too? Can you already feel your physical resistance and gut reaction?

This gut reaction is called your abreaction, your abdominal reaction. It's our body's reaction to doing something that we feel a strong resistance to, that we worry about or have an aversion to or fear of.

An abdominal reaction is when our muscles, usually our stomach muscles, contract suddenly. It's our reaction to being startled, for example, or if we fall over. Our breath stops, just for a moment. It's as if by contracting these muscles we cushion the blow and soften the pain.

This abreaction is our body's way of shouting 'stop' if we have to do something or act in a way that we resist, reject, fear or worry about; it's our body telling us it's a 'no go'. We physically contract. I call this the shock from within. This shock can cause the process to grind to a halt.

The work in this phase involves:

> Consciously focusing on your abreaction
> so that you can deal with it from within
> by taking deep breaths and relaxing.

This feels like a victory over yourself. Once you're able to manage yourself in this way, you'll feel as if you're overcoming your inner challenges.

Point 6 is a tricky phase which, even with a clear solution in sight, can cause us to suddenly come to an abrupt halt. It's like standing on the edge of a high diving board; we know there's no reason to be afraid, but our body simply refuses to jump. It's as if our whole body is contracting and all our inner worries, aversions and resistances are rising to the surface: **'I'm not doing that, no way.'**

And our mind feeds this feeling as we ask ourselves: 'Can I really do this?' 'I don't want them to think of me differently.' 'What if something goes wrong?' Your feet remain resolutely fixed to the diving board. At the thought of taking a step forward, the process comes to a halt.

Everything in you says: 'Don't do it' 'Not a chance' 'I'm out':

STOP!

This is precisely the moment that your old patterns creep back in and your defence mechanisms regain control. Your ego, with its ego worries and ego hunger, doesn't want to be pushed aside, doesn't want to budge. Your ego hunger is convinced that you can't do without your ego food. Your whole body resists, your stomach muscles clench. At the same time, this very clear physical reaction gives you the opportunity to truly understand your reaction. What's happening? And why? This moment is

your opportunity

to free yourself from what's been holding you back!
All your work in the previous phases has brought you to this point:

Your Way Out!

And now that you understand your reaction, with practice you can learn to recognise, relax, control and soften it. Every time you find the courage and determination within yourself to do this, you'll help reduce the intensity of the abreaction, a little at a time. And so the abreaction will become less and less powerful and slowly but surely will reduce its grip on you. And every time you find the courage and determination to gain control over yourself in this way, you'll feel your inner strength, self-confidence and self-assurance grow.

We must therefore once again pause at this shock point, take a deep breath and focus clearly on this inner turmoil. See it. Recognise it. Feel it. It's the only way that we can get better at dealing with it. Conquering our fears often results in a surge of energy — of courage or determination — that inspires and moves us to action.

Remember, the most important thing for you to do here is say to yourself: STOP!

Stop!	And come back to yourself.
Take a deep breath.	And relax your reflexes.
Observe your inner self.	What are you thinking, what are you feeling, what tendency or urge are you experiencing?
Play out your new alternative!	Choose consciously, experiment and learn.

Ask yourself:

- What are the triggers that can set off inner resistance, worry, aversion and/or fear in me?

- Which of the four comes up first, stronger or more often in me: the feeling of resistance, worry, aversion or fear?

- What is this resistance, worry, aversion or fear about? Where do I feel it inside me? What do I feel?

- What are my true no-go areas? What makes these such strong 'no-go's'?

- What thoughts come to mind when I think of these 'no-go's'? What are they about?

- How do I know these thoughts are true? And what if these thoughts aren't true? What then becomes possible?

- What becomes possible if I relax my 'abdominal reaction'? And how important is that to me?

- How essential is it for me to free myself from where I keep myself trapped?

- Is it an option to accept where I keep myself trapped and likely never take this step again? How does this relate to my wishes and desires at point 2?

Embrace the space

The road to
POSSIBILITIES

Once you've relaxed or conquered your abreaction in the previous phase, you move onto point 7 in the process. Relaxing our inner blockages creates an inner space and freedom. Point 7 represents this newly-created inner space. Space in which to make truly free choices.

Absolute freedom! When our fears no longer control us and no longer dominate, limit and imprison us, we're free to make our choices, both about our inner selves and the outside world.

And in this freed-up space at point 7, we shift our focus to the future. Now that we've conquered our obstacles at point 6, we can turn our gaze outwards to see what possibilities await us. What other wonderful developments can this step lead to? At this point we can let our imaginations run wild, explore best-case scenarios (rather than the worst-case scenarios at point 6) and experiment with options to our hearts' content.

With our inner obstacles relaxed, we feel a light and airy energy as our life force flows freely once again. We now feel the return of our vitality and zest for life. Inseparably linked, deep inside us, they had never actually left; they were there all along, we'd just lost contact with them for a while.

In this phase it's as if we can feel the sun once again. This free-flowing life force brings all kinds of new possibilities and ideas to the fore. It's as if we see so many more possibilities, now we've removed our 'blinkers'. As if this frees the way for creativity and inspiration.

What can, and probably will, happen at point 7 is a pleasure in trying out new things in the world around you, in new experiences. It's the pleasure of a child who plays and learns by trying out new things without worrying about the future.

It feels like positive, playful excitement. What at first seemed frightening can now feel 'enjoyably exciting'.

At point 7, we focus on our future — with the solution we identified at point 5 and looking past the obstacles at point 6. This starts out as internal process; in our minds we make plans and visualise what our future may look like. We see options and possibilities. It often begins to dawn on us that change isn't only necessary, it may even be fun!

Imagine that the chains that once bound you fall away.

What could this mean and how could it make you feel? Pure, exhilarating freedom maybe? With nothing holding you back, your life force can flow freely. You see the world through rose-tinted glasses; the sun shines brighter, you're brimming with creativity and inspiration, you feel like experimenting, playing and trying things out — the possibilities are endless.

Ask yourself:

- What do I experience after 'overcoming' point 6? What does this do to me? What do I feel?

- What space do I now suddenly see and feel?

- What new ideas, options and possibilities suddenly come into view? What now becomes possible?

- What has started flowing within me again?

- What joy, energy, creativity and inspiration do I now once more feel inside me?

- What bold steps do I now want and dare to take?

- What would be good for me to experiment with at this point? What would be good for me to learn?

- What am I curious to experience? What life experiences would I like to gain?

- What do I permit myself here? What do I want to allow myself?

- What do I now allow myself to enjoy?

- From what space or freedom do I want to benefit?

Just go for it

The road to SUBMISSION

Imagining fun possibilities is one thing. But actually taking action and standing by your decision, going for it, really committing yourself, is something else again. Up to point 8 the processes have played out primarily in your inner world, in your mind. At point 8, the time has come to bring these inner transitions into the outside world. This is a process of both surrender and action, the moment of truth has arrived: will you really take the plunge?

It's again like that moment when you're standing on the edge of the high diving board, just before you let yourself go and actually dive into the deep. Because there's no going back once you've taken the plunge. Or imagine that your new website is ready and you've got your finger on the button to send it 'live'. You feel excited and are happy that the moment has finally arrived; you want to go for it but it's still rather nerve-racking to actually 'go public'. This is the point of no return. It's the moment of true commitment.

However intense or profound your journey up to point 7 may have been, don't forget that these trials and transformations were primarily internal. It may well be that 'the outside world' hasn't noticed a difference yet. But there comes a time, namely when you reach point 8, that the transitions you've been thinking about and feeling will start to have consequences for your choices and actions in the outside world. And that's the moment of true commitment and surrender; there's no turning back.

This moment can feel quite intense and exhilarating because we don't know how people are going to react. Although our inner journey has been about detaching ourselves from the opinions of the outside world, this moment can still make us rather anxious. But it is in this moment that you are certain you want this, yet it always remains exciting.

Deep down you know that you've already passed the point of no return; you know for sure that this is what you want. This, then, is the point of real commitment.

No more thinking about it; I'm ready, I'm just going to

DO IT!

It's not only that we're taking action that's important, but also how we're taking it. Namely by standing strong; we're here — convinced and powerful. Determined, we're really going for it; nothing and no-one can stop us. We'll stick to our guns, with a clear and present mindset.

Take another deep breath, feel your feet planted firmly on the ground and tell yourself: **'I'm ready!'**

Whereas in the previous phase, at point 7, the energy was mostly lively, inspiring, free, playful and happy, at point 8 the energy has now become powerful.

This energy feels like an invisible shield, making you strong and powerful and enabling you stand proud. You can now take the necessary step forward to confront a particular situation or person, even in a situation or with a person that you used to find difficult. Bam! Unflappable, you feel like a (wo)man on a mission.

> **Ask yourself:**
>
> - What do I now truly stand for, in a way I never have before? And what am I striving for?
>
> - What do I genuinely want to commit to at point 8?
>
> - What do I now feel ready for (and strong enough) to handle?
>
> - On a scale of 0 (not at all) to 10 (fully), how committed do I feel to my choice right now?
>
> - When it comes to surrender: what is the most difficult part of surrendering for me?
>
> - What could my surrender be about?
>   What makes this so difficult for me?
>
> - What can the outside world now see, hear, feel or notice about me at this point?
>
> - What am I going to implement? If I make it concrete: what, when, with whom and how am I going to do it?
>
> - Do I need anything else for this, like support from someone else?
>
> - Can I feel the strength within myself? (Now that I have clarity about what I want to commit to and pursue?)

Hey you! Go & flow!

The road to
INTEGRATION

After the commitment, surrender and action at point 8, you return to point 9, where your journey began. But now point 9 stands for almost the opposite: when you started, this point was where you woke up from your sleep. Now that you've reached the end and are fully aware, it's time to reap and enjoy the benefits of your efforts. But also time to settle down and rest. Arriving at point 9, you feel — at first — as if you've grown wings and can fly away to a new future. At first, because point 9 is still a shock point in the transformative process, only now there's something else going on.

The end point feels comfortable — the work is done; the journey is complete. You're fully aware of what you've gone through. You feel the satisfaction of a job well done, of the steps you've taken towards personal growth, of the brave choices you've made and the challenges you've faced.

You're pleased with yourself, you feel good, you're fully conscious of the 'new you' that you've incorporated into yourself, into your life etc. You're full of good intentions. It's still new, you still need to get used to it and — you're happy. Maybe even elated.

As the end phase, point 9 is where we maybe need to take the time to let things sink in.

It's like the first time you put on a pair of new shoes. You're very pleased with them but they're still a bit stiff, a bit unfamiliar, maybe they even pinch here and there; you can feel them on your feet. Your old worn-out shoes were actually much more comfortable than these new ones. But with time, with each step, the new shoes begin to adapt to the shape of your feet. Until they're so worn in that you no longer feel them. That's exactly what's happening in this end phase, at point 9.

This settling-in phase lasts until it no longer feels like settling-in, until it no longer feels 'new'. Until you no longer have to think about your new habits. Until the new becomes 'normal'. And that's the moment that you can no longer distinguish between the 'old' and 'new'; when the change is fully integrated and has become the new 'normal'.

But until that moment, reap your reward and enjoy. You feel as if you've grown, you're in a flow, you're on your way. And while you're settling in, reaping and enjoying, it's also time for some well-earned rest. No 'difficult' actions or questions for a while.

And just like the new shoes that you soon wear in, the 'new you', your new life, your new job or whatever your transformation was about, surprisingly quickly feels normal.

One of two things may then happen: (1) we 'fall asleep' again as the new habits eventually become automatic, or (2) we not only 'fall asleep' again but, in our sleep, we fall back into old habits.

And by 'falling asleep' we again become less conscious, maybe even totally unaware, of ourselves, of the choices we make and so on. And so we once again doze and remain in this state until life wakes us up again and something comes up that we need or want to deal with. This heralds the start of yet another process and we go back to point 1.

Point 9 is therefore both the end point of a transformation process and the starting point of another journey. It's a point of connection: the point where the old and the new integrate. Behind us lie our experiences and lessons learned, before us the new unknown.

As described at the beginning of this booklet, the only thing that's permanent in the universe and in our lives is that everything is constantly in transformation. The magic wheel of life spins whether we're aware of it or not and whether we like it or not.

But with this magic wheel in your hands, from now on you'll be able to navigate new cycles ever more consciously and skilfully. Because the more often you remember to pick up and use this magic wheel, the more skilled you'll become. And over time you'll find that even the most difficult challenges will become more enjoyable; you'll find it ever easier to understand where you are in the process and what you need to do at any particular point.

And now?

This phase of integration and rest is also a great time to look back along the journey travelled, to reflect on all that has passed and all that you've discovered, learned and achieved, to evaluate what worked for you or what didn't and what you'll perhaps do differently next time.

For now, above all, it's time to be proud of yourself. To reap and enjoy the flow.

The circle is complete.

Ask yourself:

- What I changed, implemented, or did in phase 8: How did it go? How did I feel about it?

- What worked? And what didn't?

- What will I do differently next time? Or what will I do more of? Or less of?

- What successes can I celebrate from this journey?

- What benefits can I now reap? And is there any additional benefit (bycatch)?

- What am I integrating into myself, into my life?

- How's that working for me? How quickly am I adjusting?

- What are my new good habits?

- Looking back on this journey: was it easier or harder than I expected?

- Looking back on this journey: am I glad I made it? Would I recommend it to someone else?

- What am I enjoying the most right now?

Repeat the exercise we did at the beginning.
Again, first read the instructions, then carry them out.

Sit comfortably, up straight, feel your inner strength.

Close your eyes and focus on your belly.
If it helps, place a hand on your belly to help you focus.

Feel your in and out breath; the gentle expansion of your belly as you inhale and the relaxation as you exhale.

Let your breath become longer, deeper and slower.

Feel present, feel strong,
Feel comfortable and relaxed.

And when you're ready:
look at the diagram on the next page and slowly repeat, either out loud or to yourself, the words:

I AM

Let the words resonate within you,
until you can feel their vibration within your body.

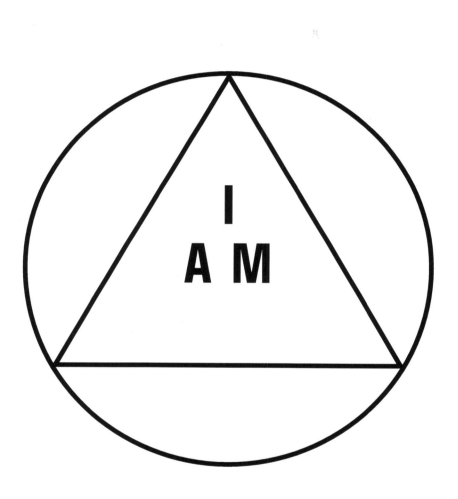

Checklist: obstacles to overcome

You can also see the 9 points on the magic wheel as internal obstacles on your path, obstacles that you want to overcome:

Point 9 Can't you or won't you wake up? Or do you wake up for a moment but decide to go back to sleep?
Then the process stops here.

Point 1 Can't you or won't you face up to your problem or the situation you're in?
Then the process stops here.

Point 2 Can't you or won't you dwell on what you really want, what you really need or what is really good for you?
Then the process stops here.

Point 3 Can't you or won't you be truly honest with yourself? About who you really are, about what really drives you, about your pitfalls?
Then the process stops here.

Point 4 Can't you or won't you let go of what no longer serves you? Are you still attached to what you now recognise as the source of your suffering?
Then the process stops here.

Point 5 Can't you or won't you rationally and honestly face the bare facts and reality — even about others?
Then the process stops here.

Point 6 Can't you or won't you tell yourself to stop, relax your inner obstacles and really start making different choices?
Then the process stops here.

Point 7 Can't you or won't you allow yourself to explore the new space you've created, to experiment with other possibilities?
Then the process stops here.

Point 8 Can't you or won't you give yourself over to turning the ideas into action and actually making the change?
Then the process stops here.

Point 9 Can't you or won't you integrate the new discoveries into yourself and into your life?
Then the process stops here.

Don't stop!

Do you want your journey to continue?
Then you can do the following:

1. Don't use this *magical wheel* just this once, and don't put this book on a shelf. Instead, give it a prominent place where you can see it. Refer to the book each time you face a dilemma, and continually ask yourself the questions from phases 9, 1, 2, and so on. Doing so will eventually become second nature, enabling you to continue learning throughout your life. You'll become increasingly adept at navigating life's challenges, thereby learning to take better care of yourself.

2. If you find it challenging to embrace this on your own and could use some support, consider joining the **'I AM THE WORK'** online community. You'll get there naturally by scanning the QR codes in this book.

Listen to the Music

The music created for each phase of this book serves a purpose.

It's not a coincidence that almost every spiritual tradition 'works' with music. Music has an impact on us as human beings — on our emotions, our thoughts, and our bodies. The vibrations of music influence our brainwaves.

Therefore, explore each phase using the corresponding track. There will come a moment when simply hearing that track can aid you in your process.

Let yourself be carried away and supported by the music of the magical wheel:

IN THE TRANSFORMATIVE TRADITION

I AM THE WORK by Enneagram Europe © 2024
Author: Jeanette van Stijn
ISBN 9789083010335

Made in the USA
Middletown, DE
24 February 2025